IRISH JOKES

IRISH JKES

G g+

Published 2019 by Geddes & Grosset, an imprint of
The Gresham Publishing Company Ltd, Academy Park, Building 4000,
Gower Street, Glasgow, G51 1PR, Scotland

Previously published as *Irish Jokes* and *Even More Irish Jokes*.

First printed 2015. Reprinted 2017, 2019.

Copyright © 2015 The Gresham Publishing Company

Illustrations by Mark Mechan

ISBN 978 1 84934 337 4

Printed and bound in the EU

Contents

Introduction

(Written by Prince Padraig Schumaker, King of the Leprechauns, Shoemaker by Royal Appointment to the Royal Court of Denmark and Holland – the little people and clogs section – and CEO of the Association of Cobblers – little clog division.)

Hello, and welcome to this brand new fantastic book of jokes.

It's not often you'll pick up a book of a leprechaun's jokes. In fact, it's unique. This is the only one. And I'll tell you why.

On a quick survey of joke books available in me local bookshop, I found not one book of jokes from a leprechaun – not even one about leprechauns. Shocking! A sad comment on the state of our world. In fact, these days even a book of Irish jokes is rare.

Not in the past and not in the golden days of comedians like Dave Allen, nor Morecambe and Wise, the Two Ronnies, nor even in the days of Father Ted, would it have been rare to find a book of Irish jokes. In those days, the shops were full of them – piled them high indeed they did. You couldn't reach the button on the pelican crossing for them, or cross a road in Cork without tripping over a stack of them, or get to the bar for a drink in Letterkenny without having to grab your ladder and clamber over humungus barricades made out of the Irish joke books.

Yes, there were plenty.

But comedy has changed. Like everything, I hear you say. Yes, everything has changed. 'Tis a pickle and a conundrum, this changing world, this one we live in.

In fact, I'd be the first to tell you that I belong to the PC Police. That's the Politically Correct Police, not the Police Constable Police, which would be an oxymoron and just plain daft. Because then I would be a leprechaun police constable in the police constable police and not a thing would get done.

There would be no sergeants or chief inspectors telling us police constables what to do. We'd be off chasing nicked bicycles all day, or worrying about which jokes had offended which people (that is humans, not witches, wizards, elves and the like – more on that in a moment), and we'd have a complete confusion about priorities and project management and annual statistics. Especially if we were plain-clothes police constables, because then no one would know to whom they should report the offensive joke or the nicked bicycle, as we'd all look the same. Unless you were a police constable leprechaun, though.

But anyway, back to me main point … humour has changed, along with fashion, politics and elves. Incidentally, we leprechauns are often confused with elves, which is odd, because since Tolkien gave them the pointy ears in *Lord of the Rings* and made them all Hollywood millionaires, we're not a bit alike. Not that we ever were alike.

Elves are from the Germanic myth tradition, whereas we leprechauns live in remote parts of Ireland and bury crocks of gold all day. Which you will know, if you took your exam along with every other leprechaun and elf in Myths: the Facts. 'Tis worth doing the government's lifelong learning programme or an OU degree – it's that fascinating.

So, anyway, back again to me point … I was thinking 'tis a heinosity that there is now no book available of Irish jokes, particularly one by a leprechaun or even by me, Padraig, King of the Leprechauns, and President of Cobblers, so I compiled me own.

I kind of missed the taunts that I was stupid or named Paddy (like everyone else in the joke books) and I missed the jokes that made fun of the English, so I decided to become a famous author with me own joke book and make a million – or a second million (as everyone knows the leprechaun is a talented chap in the money department).

Only my book of Irish jokes is in the PC tradition (politically correct not the police-constable tradition), so you won't be finding any jokes (well, maybe a few) about leprechauns, humans or religion, nuns and priests, Jesus, Mary and Joseph or Popes or even the Irish, come to that.

Neither will there be any jokes that are racist, sexist, sizeist, ageist, anti-politics, anti-miser or anti-leprechaun, for every joke in this voluminous volume has been passed by the

EU Committee for Political Correctness, and translated into 27 languages. It is the case, though, that whatever language you tell these jokes in, they are much funnier after ten pints of Guinness. Or even ten pints of Jamieson's or Bushmills, if your wallet can run to that.

It is a shame that this book can't come with a free gift (and when is a "gift" not free?) of ten pints of Guinness or three pints of me favourite – or yours – whiskey. Then you would be right in thinking me book is very funny and recommend it to all your friends.

So I want to tell you what I found out in me survey of joke books and what folk are buying these days.

I conducted this study in Dublin and Belfast and also in the online book shop that is named after a very long river that is not in Ireland. And while we are here, just what is wrong with the name Shannon.com? The Shannon is Europe's longest river after all and the whole world wants to be Irish ... Anyway, here is what you can buy a joke book on:

Cats and dogs, sex, no sex, lots of sex, insults, the law, history, doctors, death, blondes, childhood, the penis (of all things!), Mrs

Brown's Boys, Terry Wogan, women, men, mums and dads, zombies, roundabouts, the Americans, former president George W Bush (3), true stories, pub etiquette and pub stories (just why can't bears run downhill, and do we care?), the Queen, Prince Philip, love, sport, football, the office, food, the *Lord of the Rings* (of all things!), celebrities with bad hair, tractors, aunts, psychopaths, grumpy old men, and grumpy old men on holiday, big poos, kindness, pigs, chickens, being stupid, strip poker, funny signs, how to pull girls and how to pull boys.

There are even five joke books on underachievers and procrastinators but ask me how many joke books there are on leprechauns and you will find none, not one! Now then, surely 'tis an outrage that the underachievers and the procrastinators (who, after all, make terrible cobblers), they have five joke books, while we, the cobblers and leprechauns, have none.

How is it that time-wasters and George W Bush get as many as six volumes, but leprechauns nothing? Are the joke merchants sizeist? Even gnomes get a book! And 'tis a strange thing – when they come to Donegal, the tourist can buy a T-shirt, key ring, postcard, tea towel, pencil, pen and a mug with a leprechaun stamped on it (and not much more than that, be honest) but not one Irish joke book on the little leprechaun.

Sure, we are sorely misunderstood. Being a leprechaun is not all a life of sitting on a toadstool, in a meadow of four-leaf clovers, protecting the Blarney stone, wishing people "Good luck now!", and hiding from humans.

I was once cast in a film with Sean Connery (not a Bond film) about the little people, but even that misrepresented us leprechauns. We are neither wizened, all male, old, ugly, nor mythical, just as Ireland is not all a land of faerie rings and roads rising up to greet you. Mostly it is a place where we only know that summer's arrived because the rain is warm.

So let's have a warm welcome to this book of jokes and I hope by the end of it you are as sure of your own sense of humour and existence, as I am of mine!

On the Farm

A farmer returning from a trip to the market remarked:

"Well, I didn't get as much for my bull as I expected; but then, I didn't expect I would."

"By Jasus," said a farmer in earlier times, "the clergy are the very devil for collecting tithes. Be a farmer ever so poor, they'll take their tenth; Heaven help us, I would not be surprised if some of them tried to take a twentieth."

A countryman, being interviewed for a job by a strong farmer, was asked if he could live hard.

"By faith, Your Honour," he replied, "so long as Your Honour feeds me well, I could live on nothing but bread and water."

A Dubliner sent a message to a farmer he knew in the country:

"Please send bag of potatoes. If good, will send cheque."

He got a message back.

"Please send cheque. If good, will send potatoes."

A Dublin girl found herself pregnant. The father was a penniless Dutch sailor. She confided her trouble to her best friend.

"But didn't you also go to bed with young Cadogan, son of the rich farmer at Clane?

Why not place the blame on him?"

"I was thinking that myself," said the mother-to-be. "But what will come of it when the baby starts to speak and it is spouting the Dutch language?"

The farmer O'Dowd had been invited to supper by his neighbour, Cassidy.

Knowing it would be a long and late evening he took his big stable lantern with him. After a convivial session, he set off for home and reached it safely, clutching his lantern firmly all the way.

Early next morning, there was a rap on the door. He stumbled down to open it and there was his neighbour, Cassidy.

"Here's your lamp, O'Dowd," he said, "and would you mind letting me have my parrot and cage back."

"And how much of your neighbour's hay did you take?" asked the priest during a farmer's confession.

"Ah, well, your Reverence, I may as well confess to the whole stack while I'm about it. I'm going after the rest tonight."

 **A Country Life**

Pat and Mick were working hard on the Ireland Country Village In Bloom project. Pat would dig a hole and Mick would follow behind him and fill it in. They worked their way up one side of the street, then back down the other, then they moved on to the next street, working tirelessly all day without a break, Pat digging a hole, Mick filling it in again.

A visitor to the village was astonished at their hard work, but couldn't understand what they were doing. So he asked Pat, "I'm impressed by the effort you two are putting into your work, but I don't get it – why do you dig a hole, only to have your partner follow behind and fill it up again?"

Pat wiped his brow and sighed, "Well, I suppose it probably looks a bit odd because we're normally a three-person team. But today, Michael, who plants the trees, called in sick."

A poor family had no rights to the turf bog, and, at the time the neighbours were digging their peat, the son of the house sat at the door, watching the carts go by with their loads. Then, seeing one sod fall from a cart, he had an idea.

Spiking the sod of peat on a stick, he set it up in the ground. As each cart went by, he shouted, "Hey, lads, can you hit the mark?"

None of them could resist hurling a peat at the stick and by the end of the day, the lad had amassed a tidy pile without leaving his cottage door.

A blind man was out for a walk with a friend and as they crossed a field, the friend suddenly realised that there was a bull in it. A moment later the bull saw them and charged at them from behind. The friend, terrified, took to his heels, leaving the blind man walking on. The bull was so surprised to see someone calmly walking on, paying no attention, not even turning round, that his furious gallop slowed to a walk and he came up behind and with his head just nudged the blind man in the back. Immediately the man turned, stretched out his arms, seized the horns and with a twist flipped the astonished bull onto its side, where it lay in shock. The friend returned to the scene.

"Man, that was brave," he said. "I never saw anything like it."

"He's lucky," replied the blind man. "I just got the handlebars of his bicycle. If I'd got a grip of himself, I'd have given him the devil of a hiding."

Two men were passing some blackberry bushes, while the fruits were still unripe.

"It's ridiculous to call them blackberries, when they are red," said one.

His friend said, "Don't you know that blackberries are always red when they are green?"

A country gentleman ordered a new pair of leather boots from the cobbler.

As the measurements were taken, they observed one of his legs was bigger than the other, and it was agreed that the cobbler would make the boots accordingly. When they arrived, the purchaser put the big boot on the small leg and struggled in vain to get the big leg into the small boot.

Taking them back in a rage, he exclaimed, "Oh, you thief of the world, I ordered one boot bigger than the other and instead you have made one boot smaller than the other."

A country gentleman had just organised a great clear-out of his house and stables and was wondering, with his steward, what to do with the great pile of rubbish that had resulted.

"I will get a great pit dug and have it all put in there," said the steward.

"Yes, but what about the earth from the pit?" inquired his master.

"Oh, I'll get the pit made deep enough to hold that too."

It was perhaps the same steward who, having cut a hole in the back door, big enough for the cat to come in through, went on to cut a smaller one, for her kittens.

Strolling home from the pub, along a boreen far out in the country, a man heard some cries coming from the hedge. Stooping down, he saw a leprechaun with his leg caught in a rabbit snare.

"Sure, I never saw that before," he muttered. "Maybe I had too much stout."

"Help me," said the leprechaun. "Get my leg out of this."

"Are you real then?" said the man.

"As real as you're drunk," it said. "But help me, and I'll give you three wishes."

Clumsily, the man managed to loosen the wire and the leprechaun hopped free.

"Now," he said, "your wishes."

"I'd like a bottle of stout," said the man.

Immediately, it was in his hand.

"And the next wish?"

The man drained the bottle.

"And for it never to be empty," he said.

Immediately, it was full again. He gazed admiringly at it.

"And the third wish? Hurry up," said the leprechaun. "I'm late."

The man eyed him blearily.

"Just to be sure," he said, "I'll have another bottle that does the same."

Two men were walking from Mallow to Cork. Towards the end of the day they were getting very weary and footsore and one of them expressed a wish to sleep the night in a barn and go on the next day. Just then they encountered a countryman and asked him how far it was to Cork.

"Ten miles," he said.

"Ten miles!" cried the other man, turning to his friend. "Man, between the two of us, that's only five miles each. We'll walk on and be there easy as anything."

A passenger riding into Dublin on an open cart, noticing the wretched appearance of the horse as it staggered along, said to the driver:

"Really, it's cruelty to such an animal to drive it along like this."

"Your Honour," replied the driver, "it would be cruelty to a wife and seven children if I did not."

A troop of ramblers got lost and had to sleep in a cave on a hillside. In the morning their leader went out to prospect. Soon he was back.

"There is bad news and there is good news," he announced. "The bad news is that there's nothing to eat but sheep's droppings. The good news is that there's a huge supply of them."

Two unemployed men were strolling along a country lane when they came to a sign that said: "Tree Fellers Wanted".

"D'you see that, Seamus?" said Mike. "If only my brother Vinnie was here too, we'd all get a job."

"I always know when you're playing a spade," said one navvy card player.

"How's that then?"

"It's that you spit on your hands before you take it up."

The O'Carroll brothers had come across a dead horse in the field.

"What shall we do with it?" asked Michael.

"Let's raffle it," said Joseph. "€10.00 a ticket, limited sale of 200 tickets."

"But what happens when the winner finds out it's dead?" reasoned Michael.

"Sure, we'll give him his money back!" was the reply.

The Irish Abroad

Conor and Murphy are part of the crew on a cruise ship. It's their night off. They are relaxing on the upper deck.

Conor says, "Sure an' it's awfully quiet on deck tonight."

Murphy says, "Well – that's because everyone will be watching the band."

Conor says, "But there isn't a band playing tonight, Murphy."

Murphy says, "Oh yes. I definitely heard the Captain say 'a band on ship'!"

There's a Scotsman, an Englishman and an Irishman sitting in a bar in New York – homesick – hunched over their drinks – thinking about home.

"Back in ma local pub in Glasgow – The

Bon Accord," declares the Scotsman, "fer every four pints o' heavy I order, they gie me a wee hauf fer free!"

"In my pub in London," says the Englishman, "I pay for two pints of London Pride and they give me a third one free!"

"That's nuthin'," says the Irishman. "In my pub back in Dublin, you walk up to the bar, they give the first pint fer free, the second pint fer free, the third pint fer free – and then you go upstairs and you have sex for FREE!"

"Is that true?" asks the Scotsman. "Has that really happened to you?"

"Well, no," says the Irishman, "but it happens to me sister, all the time!"

An Irish priest is driving to Chicago and gets stopped for speeding. The state trooper smells alcohol on the priest's breath and then sees an empty wine bottle on the passenger seat.

He says, "Sir, have you been drinking?"

"Only water," says the priest.

The trooper says, "Then why do I smell wine?"

The priest picks up the bottle and says, "Good Lord! He's done it again!"

A soldier in an Irish regiment in the American Civil War was wounded in battle and lay on the field groaning and crying out. At last his cries so irritated another member of his company, in a similar plight, that he called out, "Damn you, stop making that noise. D'you think nobody is killed but yourself?"

A Scotsman, an Englishman and an Irishman were caught shoplifting in Paris in the year 1789 and were condemned to the guillotine. The Scotsman lay down on the scaffold with his head on the block, the executioner pulled

the handle, and nothing happened. The blade was stuck.

The Scotsman was let off and staggered away in relief. When the Englishman lay down, exactly the same thing happened.

Then it was the Irishman's turn. But before putting his head on the block, he tapped the executioner on the shoulder.

"I can see what's wrong," he said. "If you'd only tweak out that bit of twig blocking the pulley, she'll come down as sweet as you like."

An Irish visitor sat listening as an English politician ranted on in a long speech.

"I was born an Englishman, and I have lived as an Englishman and I hope to die an Englishman!" cried the speaker.

The Irishman turned to his neighbour.

"Has the man no ambition at all?" he whispered.

A beautiful Irish lady was presented at court to King George III, who politely hoped that since her arrival in London, she had been able to see all the sights and entertainments.

"Oh, yes, please your Majesty," she replied. "I believe I've seen every sight in London worth seeing, except a coronation."

On his first visit to New York, a Connemara man was astonished by the speed and volume of the traffic. Wanting to cross Fifth Avenue, he went to an intersection where a traffic cop was controlling the flow.

"Pedestrians now!" called the cop, holding his arm up to stop the cars. The man waited. The cop waved the traffic on.

After a while he held up his arm again.

"Pedestrians cross!" he shouted.

People pushed past the man, but he

stayed in place. Again the cop waved the cars on. The man looked cross.

"Fair do's," he shouted to the policeman. "That's twice in a row you've let the pedestrians through. What about the Catholics?"

An Irish couple were being shown round Texas by a guide who was anxious to extol all the virtues of his native state.

"Y'know," he said at one point, "Texas is so big that your whole country of Ireland could fit into one corner of it."

"Aye," said the husband, "and wouldn't that do wonders for the place."

An aeroplane passenger was looking rather nervous, so the stewardess came up to reassure him.

"Is it your first flight?" she asked.

"Indeed it is," he said.

"And are you feeling nervous?"

"Just a wee bit," he said. "I'm from Ahoghill, near Ballymena. No one from the village has ever been in a plane before."

After an uneventful flight, the stewardess went up to him again.

"Were you comfy, sir?" she asked.

"I told you that already," he growled. "I'm from Ahoghill in County Antrim."

A Cork man and an American were sitting at the Shannon Airport.

"I've come to meet me brother", said the man from Cork, "he's due to fly in from America in an hour's time. It's his first trip home in forty years."

"Will you be able to recognise him?" asked the American.

"I'm sure I won't," said the Cork man, "after all these years."

"I wonder if he will recognise you?" said the American.

"Of course he will, sure I haven't been away at all."

 **Nice but Dim or Just in from the Country**

A young boy and his father, from Lough Swilley, were visiting Stephen's Green Shopping Centre for the first time. They were open-mouthed by everything they saw, but especially the two shiny, silver walls that moved apart and then slid back together again all by themselves. The boy, Niall, asked, "What's that Da?"

Niall's father (never having seen an elevator) responded, "Niall, I have never seen anything like this in my life, at all, at all. I just don't know what it is."

While Niall and his father were watching in amazement, a plump elderly lady approached the moving walls and pressed a button which lit up. The walls opened and the lady walked between them into a little room beyond and she turned round and gave father and son a smile.

The walls closed and Niall and his father watched the numbers above the walls light up and go off and light up, one by one. They kept watching until the lights stopped and then the numbers began to light up again, in reverse order.

After a minute the walls opened up again and a beautiful, blonde young woman stepped out. She smiled, then moved away. The father quickly turned to Niall and excitedly said, "Niall – go get your Ma – NOW!"

An Irish labouring bricklayer made a bet with his companion and fellow labourer that he could not carry him on his hod up a ladder to the top of a high house and bring him down again safely; the bet was taken and won. As Pat, who rode upon the hod, alighted, he said, "By Jasus, he tripped once as we were coming down, and I was in hopes I should have won my bet."

A new bank robber was fully equipped.

"Remember, Seamus," the boss said, "you pull the tights over your head before we go in."

"The only trouble is," said Seamus, "I can't get them up further than me neck."

Ireland's Champion Squash Player:
Rick O'Shea

When gas was introduced, a Dubliner told her friend what an improvement it was over the coal range.

"I lit it two weeks ago," she said, "and it hasn't gone out yet."

41

Food and Drink and a Flutter

It was the day of the christening. Father O'Reilly took Michael aside and said to him solemnly, "Now then Michael – baptism is a serious thing. Are ye ready for it?"

"Yes, Father," Michael explained, "my wife has made a big 'help yourself' spread and Mrs O'Sullivan has made sandwiches and baked biscuits and cakes for everyone."

"No, Michael. That's not what I meant," Father Reilly responded. "What I mean is, are you prepared spiritually?"

"To be sure, Father," Michael replied. "There's two cases of whiskey and a case of wine, and four bottles of Baileys."

Mrs Murphy answers the doorbell and finds

her husband's best pal, Paddy, standing on the step.

"Hello Paddy, where is Dermot? He went with you to the beer factory."

Paddy shook his head. "Ah, Mrs Murphy, there was a terrible accident at the beer factory and Dermot fell into the vat of Guinness and drowned."

Mrs Murphy starts crying. "Oh don't tell me that, did he at least go quickly – did he suffer at all?"

Paddy shakes his head. "Not really – he got out three times for a pee!"

A citizen of Mallow, sitting at a Dublin supper table, heard the Sphinx mentioned and whispered to his neighbour:

"The Sphinx, who is that now?"

"A monster, man," replied the neighbour.

"You don't say so? And I thought I knew everybody who was anybody in Munster!"

For Irish Stew: take 1 pound of stewing lamb, two large onions, four pounds of potatoes, six pints of stout. Open and consume the stout. Forget the rest.

The nuns at St Mary's convent were overwhelmed to learn that old Mr O'Flaherty had left each nun a sum of money in cash to spend or give away to charity as each saw fit.

The nuns spoke animatedly and excitedly to each other about what each would do with the money. Sister Ann decided to give her share to the very first poor person she saw.

Just as she said this, she looked out the window and saw an old man leaning against the wall across the street, and he did indeed look very poor.

She ran downstairs and approached the man. He had obviously seen better days.

The nun knew he had been sent from Heaven to receive her gift.

She clasped his hand and pressed her share of the money into his hand and said, "Godspeed, my good man."

As she left, the man called out to her, "What is your name?"

"Sister Ann."

The next day, the man returned to the convent and rang the bell, with his cap in his hand. "I'm here to see Sister Ann," he said to the Mother Superior.

Mother Superior said "I'm sorry, I cannot disturb Sister Ann now. She's at prayer. Can I give her a message?"

"Yes," said the man. "Give her this and tell her Godspeed came in at 13 to 1 in the 2.30 at Cork."

On a cold winter night, Red Hanrahan went out to buy himself a half-bottle of whiskey. Stowing it away in his hip pocket, he set off home again. But on the icy road he slipped and fell. As he got to his feet, he felt something liquid trickling down his leg.

"Please God," he said, "let it be blood."

"Drink is a curse," announced the priest solemnly to his parishioners. "It makes you quarrel with your neighbours. It makes you get your gun out to shoot the landlord. And it makes you miss him."

Murphy and Michael are at the Galway races. Michael taps the side of his nose and whispers to Murphy "Do you want the winner of the next race?"

Murphy replies, "No thanks, I've only got a small garden."

A coach party from St Mary's Women's Guild is on a mystery tour and decides to run a sweepstake to guess where they were going.
  The driver won.

Michael and Mick are walking down the road and Michael's got a bag of cream cakes in his hand. Michael says to Mick, "If you can guess how many cream cakes are in my bag, you can have them both."

The worst thing about him is, when he's not drunk, he's sober.

God, Death, Funerals, Graveyards and the Pearly Gates

There were six old pals from County Claire playing poker in O'Brien's Bar when Michael Murphy loses all his money in a single hand, clutches his chest and collapses at the card table.

The ambulance comes – but there's nothing can be done. Murphy is pronounced dead.

The bartender looks around and asks, "Well me boys, someone's to tell Michael's wife. Who is it going to be?"

They solemnly draw straws. The shortest one is in Patrick's hand. The pals tell him to be tactful, discreet and gentle and not make an awful situation any worse for Mrs Murphy. They put the money pot from the night's game into a bag and hand it to Patrick.

Patrick goes to Murphy's house and knocks on the door. Mrs Murphy comes to the door and asks what he wants.

Patrick stumbles over his words at first but blurts out "Your husband just lost a lot of money at poker and is afraid to come home."

"Well you just go back and tell him to drop dead!" says Murphy's wife.

"I'll go tell him right now, Mrs Murphy," says Patrick, bag in hand.

Pat and Mick were walking home from O'Brien's Bar on Halloween night. They took the shortcut through the cemetery as usual. Not far from the gate, they were startled by a tapping noise coming from within the new part of the graveyard.

They found an old man with a hammer and chisel, chipping away at one of the headstones. They were petrified.

"Jasus, man, you frightened the life out of us," Pat shrieked. "You scared us half to death – we thought you were a ghost!

"What are you doing working here at this time of night?" shouted Mick.

"My friends are such numpties!" the old man replied. "They misspelled my name and I'm here to correct it!"

An Irishman was beside himself with frustration at not being able to find a parking space in Boyd's car park.

He prayed – "Lord, I can't stand this any longer. If you open up a space for me, I swear on my mother's grave that I'll give up drinking whiskey and I'll to go to church every Sunday."

Suddenly, the clouds parted and a beam of sunlight shone down onto an empty parking space. Without hesitation, the man said, "It's all right, Lord. Never mind, I found one."

"How old was the deceased?" asked an observer at a funeral.

"Oh, very old," replied one of the mourners. "He was eighty-five."

"That's not so old," returned the other. "Why, if my own father was alive today, he'd be a hundred and twelve."

May you never live to see your wife a widow.

May you be in Heaven for half an hour before the Devil knows you're dead.

May your friends have fine weather for your funeral.

Better to be a coward for a moment than a dead hero for the rest of your life.

An Irishman, it's said, will die before he lets himself be buried outside Ireland.

The parish atheist died and the priest came to pay his condolences to the household. As he left, he commented to himself:

"Sad, really. There he was, all dressed up, and nowhere to go."

Murphy opened the daily newspaper and was astonished to read in the obituary column that he had died. He immediately phoned his boss, Mr Finnegan.

"Did you see the paper?" asked Murphy. "They say I died!"

"Yes, I saw it!" replied Finnegan. "Where are ye callin' from?"

A clergyman was reading the burial service in the course of a funeral.

Coming to the lines which refer to "our dear brother or sister", he realised that he had forgotten the sex of the departed, and whispered to a man standing close by, "Is it a brother or a sister?"

"Ah, neither," said the man, "just a cousin."

Danny was walking by the pub when he saw a bright and shiny new motorbike parked outside it, with the key still in the lock. Thinking he would like to try a ride, he wheeled it quietly away to a place where the sound of the engine would not be heard, started it up and away he went. He was having a fine spin, but soon he felt cold. So he stopped and put his jacket on back to front and turned his cap round with its peak to the back, to keep the wind off him. Then he set off again. Going faster now, he lost control of the machine, hit the bank of the road and went flying off, just where some people were at work in a field. The accident was duly reported to the Gardai, and an officer came to the scene.

"Was it instant death, then?" he asked the witnesses.

"No, he was alive lying in the road," said one. "But as soon as we set his head straight, he died."

Father O'Leary was a doughty champion of Catholic doctrine who nevertheless had many friends and admirers in the Church of Ireland. After they had been guests at the same dinner, the lawyer, John Philpot Curran, not a great churchgoer, said to him:

"I wish you were St Peter."

"Why so, counsellor?" asked the priest.

"Because you might let me in, as master of the keys."

"It were better for you that I had the keys of the other place," said O'Leary, "for then I could let you out."

When her husband returned home late with a black eye, a broken nose and a split lip, Mrs Sullivan was shocked, but not surprised.

"What happened?" she asked.

"I got it fightin' with Pat Dugan," he said.

"Ye big stiff," said his wife. "Why, Pat Dugan's just a little shrimp of a fellow. How could you let a miserable weakling like him do that to you?"

"Hush, woman," said Sullivan. "Speak no ill of the dead."

The only plumber in Dublin to charge reasonable rates died. Due to an administrative mix-up, he was sent to Hell. Eventually it was realised in Heaven that there was an honest plumber in the wrong place.

St Peter got on the hot line to Satan.

"Have you got an honest plumber there?"

"Yes."

"Well, send him up. He's ours."

"You can't have him."

"What do you mean?"

"I'm getting him to put in air conditioning. It's going to be really cool down here soon."

"Send him up!" shouted St Peter. "Or we'll sue."

The voice at the other end laughed.

"You'll sue? And just where do you think you'll get hold of a lawyer?"

"When I die," said Tim O'Donovan to his best friend, "I want you to get a bottle of the finest Irish whiskey and pour it over my grave. Will you do that?"

"Surely," said his friend. "You won't mind if I pass it through the kidneys first, will you?"

Literature, Poetry and Verse

Alternative Lines from Irish Literature

Believe me, if all these endearing young
   charms,
Which I gaze on so fondly today,
Were to change by tomorrow and fleet in my
   arms,
I would run like the blazes away.

Near to Banbridge town, in the County
Down, one morning in July,
Down a boreen green came a sweet colleen,
And she spat right in my eye.

There's a dear little plant that grows in our
  isle
And if you smoke it you'll end up in jyle.

The harp that once through Tara's halls
The soul of music shed,
Now hangs quite mute on Tara's walls –
They've karaoke instead.

Down by the Salley Gardens my love and I
  did meet;
She'd stepped on something squishy with
  her little snow-white feet.

I once loved a boy, just a bold Irish boy,
Who'd come and who'd go at my request;
But mostly I would ask him to go,
Because of his smelly vest.

Mellow, the moonlight its shine is beginning;
Close by the window young Eileen is sinning.

Kathleen Mavourneen! The grey dawn is
    breaking,
The horn of the hunter is heard on the hill;
Wake up, my girl, it's time you were taking
Your regular morning-after pill.

In Dublin's fair city, where girls are so pretty,
A striking exception was Molly Malone.

Oft in the stilly night, ere slumber's chain has
    bound me,
I find the eiderdown has slipped off from
    around me.

Oh, Danny Boy, the pipes, the pipes are
    calling,
From glen to glen, and down the
    mountainside,
The noise they make is truly quite
    appalling,
'Twould make a music-lover run and
    hide.

Great Short Books of Our Time

Arm Movements for Irish Dance

Ireland: Centre of World Cricket

Hurling for Softies

The Kerryman as Romantic Lover

Banana-Growing in Your Irish Garden

Collected Christmas Goodwill

Messages from the Moderator of the Free
Presbyterian Church to His Holiness the
Pope

The Irishman's Guide to Helping About the
House

The Guide to Irish Motorway Service Stations

Things to Do on a Dry Day in Donegal

In Praise of Country Bungalows

More Wisdom

In some parts of Ireland the sleep that knows no waking is followed by the wake that knows no sleeping.

What's the difference between a Kerry wedding and a Kerry wake?
There's one drunk less at the wake.

Children are the curse of this country – especially if you don't have any.

Everything here is perfectly abnormal.
(A Dublin saying)

What's the world to a man, if his wife is a widdy?

The most popular speaker is the one who sits down before he gets up.

God bless the Holy Trinity.
(A motto seen on a banner in a Dublin religious procession)

Bishop Woodward of the Church of Ireland had made an attack on the doctrine of Purgatory, upon which Father O'Leary observed:

"However clamorous a mitred divine might be about a Popish purgatory, he may perhaps go further, and fare worse."

Country Proverbs

When the cat is out, the dog is in.

Where there's a will, there's a won't.

When the wine is in, people drink it.

Man proposes, and woman refuses.

A stitch in time loses the race.

People who live in glass houses grow the best tomatoes.

Every cloud has a silver lining with a hole in it.

When the drop is inside, you don't care if the sense is outside or not.

The cracked pitcher is the one that would otherwise have been a valuable antique.

He who gets a name for rising early finds himself having to make the porridge.

A word to the wise earns a punch on the nose.

Sufficient unto the day is the apple thereof.

Country Proverbs

A fool and his money rush in where angels fear to tread.

Beware of a tight man and a loose dog.

The Long Arm of the Law

O'Callaghan was from a powerful criminal family in the province of Munster and he was on trial again for armed robbery. The case lasted for five weeks.

The jury foreman eventually came out and announced, "Not guilty."

"That's grand!" shouted O'Callaghan. "Does that mean I can keep the money?"

"Daniel Sean O'Leary," said the judge, looking sternly at the defendant, "it's alcohol and alcohol alone that's responsible for your present sorry, sorry state!"

"Thank you, Your Honour. I'm very glad to hear you say that," replied O'Leary, with an obvious sigh of relief. "Everybody else says it's all my fault!"

There's a man charged with a double murder in court in Dublin.

The judge summarises, "Patrick Murphy O'Brien, you are charged with beating your cousin to death with a hammer."

There's a disturbance at the back of the courtroom and someone shouts out, "You bastard!"

The judge continues, "Patrick Murphy O'Brien, you are also charged with beating your uncle to death with a hammer."

There is a further disturbance at the back of the courtroom and another shout, "You dirty rotten bastard!"

The judge calls for order and asks the man at the back of the courtroom, now restrained by court officers, "Sir, I can understand your anger and frustration at these terrible crimes, but there will be no more outbursts from you, or you'll be charged with contempt. Is that clear?"

The man is released from the grip of the officers and stands tall and says, "I'm sorry,

Your Lordship, but for fifteen years I've lived next door to that O'Brien eejit and every time I asked to borrow a hammer, he said he didn't have one."

A member of the landed gentry was stopped for speeding on the motorway to Dublin Airport.

"Do you know who I am?" the man protested. "I am a member of one of Ireland's oldest families."

"So what?" said the cop. "We're not after ya for breeding from."

Sentenced by the warship's captain to a dozen lashes, a seaman fled up into the rigging of the vessel and clung to the mast-head, where no one could reach him.

"Come down, you rascal," roared the

Captain. "Come down this instant or I'll give you two dozen."

"I won't," called the seaman. "I won't come down, no, not if you was to make it four dozen."

A man was in court for non-payment of maintenance to his estranged wife.

After hearing the case, the judge said, "I have decided to give her an extra ten pounds a week."

"Bless Your Honour," said the man. "You're very kind to do that. Maybe I'll send her a few shillings myself, as well."

"Your Honour, we find the man who stole the mare, 'Not guilty'."

"What became of old Dan McGrew?"
   "Didn't you hear? He was sentenced to be hanged but he saved his life by dying in prison."

What is an alibi?
An alibi is the ability to be in two places at once.

Sentencing a persistent armed robber to life imprisonment for stealing a priceless, solid-gold cuckoo clock, the exasperated judge remarked to the criminal:
"By grasping at time, you have enabled yourself to attain eternity."

 # Love and Marriage

There were three brothers. The first brother married a Greek girl. He told her that she was to do the dishes and house cleaning. It took a few days, but on the third day he came home to find a sparklingly clean house and all the dishes washed and put away in the cupboard.

The second brother married a girl from the Philippines. He told his wife that she was to do all the cleaning. It took a couple of days, but on the third day he came home to see a clean house and dishes washed and put away in the cupboard.

The third brother married a girl from Dublin. He ordered her to keep the house cleaned, dishes washed, the grass cut, the washing done and demanded hot meals on the table at 7 o'clock sharp every day. The first day he didn't see anything, the second day he didn't see anything either but by the third day, the swelling had gone down, and he could see out of his left eye and his arm was healed enough that he could make himself a sandwich and load the washing machine. He still experiences some discomfort when he urinates.

Paddy's wife was fed up to the back teeth complaining about her husband spending all his spare time in the bar, so one night he suggested he take her along with him.

"What'll you have?" he asked.

"Oh, I don't know. The same as you I suppose," she replied.

Paddy ordered a large Jack Daniel's and a half of Guinness and threw both in one. His wife watched him, then took a sip from her own glass and spat it out. "Paddy, that's TERRIBLE! What a disgusting taste," she coughed. "How you can drink this stuff!"

"Well, there you go," cried Paddy. "You think I'm out enjoying myself every night!"

Collins and Clarke are in the bar on Christmas Eve. "So, did you figure out what to buy your Missus for Christmas?" asked Collins.

"I sure have, she decided it for me," answered Clarke. "She said she wanted something with diamonds in it, so I've bought her a pack of cards."

"Will you hurry up!" called Mr Corcoran to his wife. "If you don't get a move on we'll be late."

"Will you stop your nagging," she shouted. "I've been telling you for the past hour – I'll be ready in a minute."

Terence Molloy was a great enthusiast for the drink. Every evening he would go down to the pub and he would come back drunk. This was very vexing to his wife. She was at her wit's end for what to do. Then she had an idea. Terence always took a short-cut home, on a path that led through the churchyard.

She decided that she'd give him a scare that would get him off the drink forever.

She got hold of a pair of goat horns, a devil-mask and an old red curtain, and made them into a costume for herself.

Then, late one moonlit evening, she disguised herself in this outfit and hid behind a tall tombstone. In due course Terence came along, stumbling slightly and singing in a slurred voice. His wife stepped out from behind her hiding place, ready to give him a terrible warning. But Terence rocked back on his heels and eyed the apparition.

"I am the Devil!" she roared.

"Pleased to meet you," said Terence. "We're sort of related. I'm married to your sister."

Michael is home alone watching TV when the doorbell rings. When he opens the door, there are two Gardai, holding their hats respectfully in their hands.

They ask to come in. One of them asks if he is married and, if so, whether they can see a picture of the wife.

Michael replies "Of course" and picks up their wedding picture from the sideboard.

The officer looks carefully at the picture and then gravely says, "I'm sorry sir, but it looks like your wife's been hit by a truck."

Michael replies "I know, but she has a great personality, she's a great cook, and she lets me go and play golf whenever I want!"

"Oh, Maureen, why won't you marry me?" demanded Kevin, then, suddenly suspicious, "There isn't anyone else, is there?"

"Oh, Kevin," sighed Maureen. "If only there could be."

"Tell me this," said Mr Kelly to Mr Keogh, "what is it that we have wives for?"

After some thought, Mr Keogh said, "Well, it's for the things that go wrong that you can't blame the government for."

Doolan was looking particularly miserable.

"My wife told me today that she believes in free love," he said to his friend Devane.

"Well, that's all right, mine does too," said Devane.

"But you always seem to be such a devoted couple," said Doolan.

"And so we are," said Devane. "She wouldn't dream of charging me."

"How's your wife?"
"She's very sick."
"Oh, dangerous?"
"No, she's too weak to be dangerous."

He: "If I was to propose to you, Kathleen,
  would you say 'Yes'?"
She: "If you thought I would say 'Yes', Danny,
  would you propose to me?"

Anna accompanied her husband, Dylan, to
the doctor's surgery.

After Dylan had a full examination, the
doctor asked to speak to Anna alone. He
said, "Your husband is suffering from a

very severe stress disorder. If you don't look after him your husband will die. Every morning, make him a healthy breakfast. Be nice to him at all times. For lunch make him a three-course meal. For dinner prepare some poached fish. Something light. Don't burden him with household chores. Don't discuss any problems with him, it will only make his stress even worse. And most importantly, don't nag. If you can do this for the next year, I think Dylan will make a full recovery."

On the way home, Dylan asked Anna, "And what did the doctor say?"

"He said you're going to die," she replied.

A wife had brought money to the marriage and never allowed her husband to forget it. When a visitor remarked on the piano, she said, "If it wasn't for my money, we wouldn't have it."

When the visitor admired a picture on the

wall, she said, "Yes, it was my money bought us that."

When the visitor complimented them on the new silk curtains, she said, "If it wasn't for my money, they wouldn't be here."

"If it wasn't for your money," muttered her husband, not quite quietly enough, "I wouldn't be here either."

As the groom stood beside his bride-to-be, the priest observed that his eyes were crossing and uncrossing, that he could scarcely stand upright, and that a powerful odour of drink was coming from him.

"I can't possibly marry you in this state," he said severely. "He'll have to come back when he's sober."

"Oh, please Father, carry on," she cried. "He won't COME back, if he's sober."

Mrs Milligan went to see a solicitor in her home town.

"I want to divorce my husband."

"I see," said the solicitor. "Do you have a grudge?"

"No," said Mrs Milligan. "We keep the car on the pavement."

"Does your husband beat you up?"

"No," she replied, "it's me that's always up first making him a cup o' tea."

The solicitor sighed. "Does he go in for any, ah, funny business? You know, in bed?"

"The man couldn't crack a joke to save his life," said Mrs Milligan.

"Well, what are your grounds?" asked the solicitor.

"Grounds? We have no grounds. We live on the third floor."

"Mrs Milligan," said the solicitor, "I'm trying to establish why you want to divorce your husband."

"It's because he's an impossible man to hold an intelligent conversation with."

A couple were writing begging letters when they heard their lottery numbers read out on the television.

"We've won a million pounds, Dermot!" shrieked his wife.

"Okay, okay," said Dermot. Just finish off the letters."

Mrs Grundie had been to the dressmaker's to be measured for a new skirt.

"What did she say about that big bum of yours?" asked Mr Grundie.

"Your name was never mentioned," she said coldly.

"Dennis," said his wife, "did you see that fine new hat and coat Mrs Culley was wearing in church today?"

"No, I did not," said Dennis. "I'm afraid I was dozing off most of the time."

"Dennis!" exclaimed his wife. "A fat lot of good it does you to go to church."

A priest was talking encouragingly to a couple who were well known for quarrelling all the time.

"Why, look at your cat and dog," he said. "They get on better than you two do."

"Try tying them together, and then see," said the man.

On their wedding night, Peggy and Dermot retired early to the honeymoon suite. Peggy was soon in bed, but she was surprised to see Dermot sitting down, fully dressed, in a chair.

"Aren't you coming to bed, dearest?" she asked.

"No fears," said Dermot. "My mother said this would be the best night of my whole life and I'm not going to bed and missing any of it."

Mrs O'Reilly came back from her Gourmet French Cookery class. She tells her husband Paddy she is going to prepare him a special meal and he is to go down to Sean's Market and buy two dozen escargot, which she explains to him are snails. She tells him to come straight back, not to stop at every pub on the way, because she wants to have dinner sharp. Paddy buys the snails as instructed, and is on his way home but his route back takes him right by the door of The Labour's Rest pub. Just one he says to himself. Well, perhaps another he says after having the first. The company is good, the tales are tall, and Paddy finds himself

having three or four and four becomes
five. As Paddy heads home he realises it
has become dark and knows his wife will
be waiting and angry. As Paddy opens the
gate to home the porch light comes on and
he hears the door begin to open. Paddy
empties the bag of snails on the ground and
says in a loud voice "Come on now my lads!
You're almost there."

Walking into the pub, Patrick said to the
bartender, "Pour me a large one, Sean. I just
had another barney with the little woman."

"Oh," said Sean. "And how did this one
end up?"

"Well I'll tell ya now – when it was all over,"
Patrick replied, "she herself came to me on
her hands and knees, she did."

"You don't say? Now that's a bit different
from last time! What did she say?"

Patrick replied, "She said, 'Come out from
under that bed, you gutless wee man'!"

Murphy had asked Mr O'Toole for the hand of his daughter in marriage.

"And can you support a family?" asked O'Toole.

"I think so," replied Murphy.

"Well. There's eight of us, you know," said the future father-in-law.

The Things People Say

When a lady observed one day how bright and beautiful the sunshine was, a friend of hers replied:

"That's all very well, but the moon is much more useful. It gives us light at night, when we really need it; the sun just shines all day when it's broad daylight anyway."

"Have you seen Rafferty lately?"

"Well, yes and no."

"How do you mean, yes and no?"

"Well, I saw someone I thought was him, and he saw someone he thought was me, but when we got up to each other we saw it wasn't either of us."

"When I first saw you, I thought it was you, but now I see it is your brother."

The auctioneer declared:
"Every item on sale here will be sold to the highest bidder, unless someone else offers more."

"Madam," said the serving girl, "there's a poor man at the door with a wooden leg."
   "Well, tell him I don't need any wooden legs today."

"I saw a really beautiful dress in that boutique," said Maureen. "It would have fitted me perfectly, if I could have got into it."

When a friend of Captain O'Neill fell ill, the Captain warned him:

"Do not send for Dr Slane."

"Why not?" asked the invalid.

"Well, when I was ill, he came to see me, and filled me that full of potions and powders, that I stayed ill for a good two weeks after I was well again."

When a lady was buying a dress length, she asked the merchant if it was durable stuff.

"It will wear for ever, madam, and make you a petticoat afterwards," he replied.

At the end of a sociable evening, a guest was looking for his coat.

"Sure, you're wearing it," said his host.

"Why, so I am," he said, looking down. "I'm so glad you told me, or I'd have gone home without it."

I would have been a man of considerable property, if only my father had never entered the family.

One fine day, two old men were sitting on a seat in the market square.

"It's fine weather that's in it," one remarked.

"Indeed," said the other. "Such grand weather, I'm sorry I'm not still working, so that I could take the day off."

One man is as good as another, and often a damn sight better.

Surveying her new class, the teacher said, "All I want out of you is silence, and not too much of that, either."

A man sitting in a restaurant said to his companion, "I'm nearly sure that the man over there in the corner is my old school friend, Haggerty."

"Why don't you go over and say hello?" said his companion.

"I don't think I will," said the man. "You see, the thing is, he's so shy he would feel awkward if it turned out he was the wrong man."

Looking round the greybeards in the village pub, the visitor asked:

"How old is the oldest man in the place?"

"Oh, we don't have an oldest man any more," said one of the locals. "He died last week."

A particularly lean citizen, encountering a similarly shaped friend, said: "I have just been speaking to our old friend, Terence O'Hare. He is grown so thin, I scarcely knew him; you may be thin and I may be thin but, by faith, he's thinner than both of us put together!"

Mr Kogan, hammering at the door:
"Is it dead or alive you are in there?"
Mr Grogan, from within:
"It's neither I am, but sleepin'."

"Is it very noisy where you live?"
"I'll say it is. It's so noisy we only ever get any peace when a plane coming into the airport drowns out the noise of the traffic on the motorway."

"If you don't leave me alone," shouted Doreen to Dermot, "I'll go and find someone who will!"

The colonel of an Irish regiment called up a private soldier who had captured three enemy soldiers in battle. After commending his bravery he asked, "And how did you manage to capture three men, single-handed?"

"Well, sir," replied the soldier, "I managed to surround them, so they just had to surrender."

Dolan and Rafferty were fighting, and Dolan appeared to be getting the better of it.

"When you're beaten," said Dolan, "you should say you've had enough."

"If I have the strength to say I've had enough," gasped Rafferty, "then I'm not beaten yet."

"How can you tell your twin boys apart, Mrs Sullivan?" asked a neighbour.

"Oh, it's not difficult. If I put my finger in wee Sean's mouth and he bites me, I know it's wee Pat."

Paddy couldn't believe it. Saturday morning at 8.30 am and there's a knock at the door and he's confronted by a debt collector.

"Why haven't you made any payments on the double glazing you had fitted," demanded the debt collector.

"Don't ask me," said Paddy. "Ask your salesman. He said the stuff would pay for itself in six months!"

"Can I have a pair of kippers?" said Thomas to the fishmonger.

"I'm sorry, Thomas. We haven't got a pair left," said he.

"That's all right," said Thomas. "Give me two odd ones, she won't know any difference!"

 **Smart Ass**

A stranger stops Ted in Dublin and asks for the quickest way to Cork.

Ted says, "Are you on foot or in your car?"

The stranger says, "In the car."

Ted says, "That's the quickest way."

A small boy, when asked how old he and his brother were, replied, "He's ten and I'm eight, but in two years' time I'll have caught him up."

Two gentlemen were walking down Grafton

Street in Dublin, just as the maids were out mopping the doorsteps. One of them placed her bucket in such a way that one of the men inadvertently kicked it.

"Oh, my dear man," said his friend. "I am sorry to see you have kicked the bucket at last."

"Not at all," said the man. "I have only turned a little pail."

"Martin, can you spell 'paint'?" asked the teacher.

"Which colour, miss?" he asked.

A Tralee man came to Dublin for a few days and decided to get his hair cut at a smart hairdresser's. He went into the salon and asked, "How much is a haircut?"

"Haircuts start at fifteen pounds."

Wow, he thought, I didn't expect it to be that much. "What about a shave?" he asked.

"That would be five pounds."

He sat down in the chair. "Shave my head, then," he said.

Arriving at Knock Airport, an American visitor saw a stall with "Unusual Irish Souvenirs" over it and went across to have a look. The first thing that caught his eye was a human skull, labelled "St Patrick's Skull – a unique opportunity to acquire this remarkable relic. Guaranteed Genuine."

"How much?" asked the visitor, and though he was disconcerted to find out the price, he paid up and went off with the skull carefully wrapped in a copy of *The Knock Weekly Knocker*. He took the skull home, and treasured it for many years. Much later in life, he revisited Ireland and went again to Knock.

Seeing the "Unusual Irish Souvenirs" stall still there, he went to look, and was more than surprised to see "St Patrick's Skull" again on sale.

"But I bought that from you twenty years ago!" he protested to the stallholder.

The man scratched his head.

"The thing was," he said. "What you bought was St Patrick's skull, all right. But yours was when he was grown up. This one here is from St Patrick when he was just a boy."

Three priests from the West were travelling by train to a meeting in Dublin.

To while away the time, one said, "We've known each other a long time, but we don't really know each other very well. Why don't we each tell one thing about ourselves that we keep a dark and deadly secret? Even men of the cloth can have a human weakness. We'll feel better for confiding it, and we'll know one another all the better."

Seeing the other two look rather reluctant, he went on, "I'll start. All my parishioners think I'm a most abstemious man, but every now and then I go on the bottle and get drunk for days at a time. They all think I'm on holiday."

This prompted the next one to say, "My own weakness is gambling. Every now and then I can't resist putting money on the horses. I'm afraid that's where the money for the choir outing went."

They turned to the third priest.

"And what about you?"

"Me?" he said, with a serene smile. "My only weakness is that sometimes I just can't help gossiping and giving away things people tell me in confidence."

Teacher: What is the male of a cow?
Boy: Grass.

At the Limerick Fair a countryman bought
a mare from a horse-dealer. The dealer

promised him that the animal was sound in wind and limb, and faultless in all respects. After buying the horse, the purchaser discovered that it was blind in one eye, and almost so in the other.

Returning to find the dealer, he complained bitterly about being tricked by lies.

"Not a word of a lie is there in it," said the dealer, refusing to repay the price. "The poor creature is almost blind, that is true. But that is not her fault: it is her misfortune."

A special fund had been organised by the new priest to pay for mending the leaky roof of the parish church. In charge was the treasurer, Mike Nolan. One evening the priest met Mr Nolan and found him definitely the worse for wear.

"Mike," he said, "have you been at the pub?"

"No, Father," said Nolan. "I've been collectin' the sub-sub-whatd'youcallums for the church roof, an' everyone I called on insisted on me havin' a glass of whiskey with them."

"But surely not everyone in the parish is a whiskey drinker?"

"Oh, no, Father. I sent my wee boy round to collect from them that isn't."

An American visitor had recently arrived at Shannon, and had hired a taxi driver to show him some of the sights. As they drove along the roads, he gave the driver some helpful information about his own country.

"Of course you're in the old world here," he said. "Everything takes a long time. I know. Back home, we can build a twenty-storey building in a fortnight. Here I guess it would take you two years."

The driver hunched his shoulders and said nothing. By and by they came in sight of the bulk of Bunratty Castle.

Looking out of the window, the American whistled. "What's that?" he asked.

"I don't know," said the taxi driver. "It wasn't there when I came by here yesterday."

A well-known RTE sports commentator had to go to hospital for an operation.

Despite his jolly screen personality, he turned out to be a nightmare patient. He shouted at the nurses, was rude to his fellow-patients, and questioned the doctors' knowledge, qualifications, and, when they weren't there, their parentage.

He asked the lady with the library books if she had any porn. He found fault with absolutely everything.

One morning, a medical auxiliary whom he had not seen before came to take his temperature.

"Get on with it, woman," he said.

"No, no," she said. "I have to take it from the other end. Doctor's orders."

After loud protest, he submitted to having his pyjama trousers pulled down, and the thermometer inserted in his anus.

"Stay like this for three minutes," she said. "I'll be right back."

Time passed.

He remained with his bottom in the air.

After much more than three minutes he shouted, "What's going on?"

There was a sound of footsteps and the ward sister appeared. She looked at him and gasped.

"What's the matter?" he snarled. "Haven't you seen someone having his temperature taken before?"

"Not with a plastic daffodil," she said.

The holidays were over and the teacher asked the class what they had done that they had liked best. Tim eagerly put up his hand. "Miss, we visited our cousins in Carrigaline!"

"Well, Tim," says the teacher, "that sounds wonderful and can you tell us all how to spell Carrigaline?"

Tim paused, scratched his head, and then declared with a big smile, "Em, well Miss er, now, come to think of it, I liked Cork better!"

Leprechauns

A woman was sitting at a bar in Dublin, enjoying an after-work cocktail with her girlfriends when a little leprechaun walked into the bar. He was an exceptionally tall, handsome, extremely sexy leprechaun, as leprechauns go.

In fact, for once, this leprechaun was so striking that the woman could not take her eyes off him. The young-at-heart, little (but exceptionally tall for a little leprechaun, as leprechauns go) leprechaun noticed her overly attentive stare, and walked directly towards her. (As all leprechauns, and men, will.)

Before she could offer her apologies for staring so rudely, he jumped up onto a bar stool, leaned over and whispered, "I'll do anything, absolutely anything you want me to do, no matter how kinky, for 50 euros, on one condition." Then he winked and said, "As I'm rich, 'cos I have a crock of gold at the end of my very long rainbow (wink, wink), it's only the 50 euros!"

Flabbergasted, the woman asked what that condition was. The little leprechaun, who was exceptionally tall and growing taller and more handsome by the minute, replied, "You have to tell me what you want me to do in just three words. Three words, mind! Can you do it? Most women can't, and I win!"

And then he laughed in a rather ugly way and winked cheekily again.

Well … the good woman of Dublin, out

with her pals, considered this for a moment and then slowly took 50 euros from her purse, which she pressed into the wee leprechaun's hand along with her business card.

The leprechaun shifted excitedly on his bar stool and his little legs, which were longer than average for an exceptionally tall and sexy and handsome leprechaun (as leprechauns go, or come, as it were), took the euros and the card and looked up into her eyes. And the very beautiful Dublin girl leaned towards him and looked deeply into his eyes. The leprechaun crinkled the notes, breathed slightly breathlessly, and waited, his gorgeous eyes (for a leprechaun) on stalks.

And the Dublin lass said, lingeringly and slowly, "CLEAN MY HOUSE!"

A very short man, who can hardly see over the dashboard, is speeding along a narrow road in his BMW, up from the Ring of Kerry, when a beautiful blonde woman comes hurtling round the corner in a Nissan Micra, with an English number plate. He swerves to avoid her, but as she passes she leans out the window and screams "MIDGET!"

Insulted and angry, the man turns and yells back "ENGLISH EEJIT!" as he reaches the bend and crashes into a leprechaun.

Two leprechauns have a bet to settle so they go to a convent. When Mother Superior answers the door, the first leprechaun says, "We want to ask you a question. Are there any nuns in your convent that are my size?"

"No, little man, there are no nuns in my convent that are your size."

"Alright then. Are there any nuns in all of Ireland, that are my size?"

"No, little man, there are no nuns in all of Ireland that are your size."

"All right then. One more question. Are there any nuns in all of the world, that are my size?"

"No, little man, I am quite sure there are no nuns in all of the world that are your size!"

"Okay then."

The second leprechaun starts laughing and says, "You see, I told you she was a penguin!"

A leprechaun rushes in to see his doctor, completely frazzled.

He shouts, "Doctor! Would you just take a look at me? When I woke up this morning, I looked at myself in the mirror and saw my hair falling out, my skin all wrinkled and wizened, my eyes bulging out and I looked like I was 308 years old! What's WRONG with me?"

The doctor looks him over, and calmly says, "Well, I can tell you that there's nothing wrong with your eyesight!"

A female leprechaun gets on the bus in Letterkenny with her baby called Jo. As she pays for her ticket, the bus driver says, "Ugh! That's the ugliest baby I've ever seen."

The female leprechaun jumps up to the seat, and sits down, furious and fuming.

She says to a man sitting next to her, "That driver's just insulted me!"

The man says, "You shouldn't take that. You tell him off – go ahead, I'll hold your monkey."

A leprechaun joined a dating agency and went out on a series of dates that didn't work out.

Irate, he went back to the woman who ran the agency and said, "Have you not got someone on your books who doesn't care what I look like or what height I am or what job I have, and has a nice, big pair of boobs?"

So she checked on her computer and said, "Actually, we do have one person, but unfortunately it's you."

A ventriloquist is telling Irish jokes in a pub, when an irate Irishman stands up and says, "You're makin' out we're all dumb and stupid. I oughtta punch you in the nose."

"I'm sorry sir, I ... "

"Not you," says the Irishman. "I'm talking to that little fella sitting on your knee."

 **Politics**

An aging man lived alone in his home in southern Ireland. His only son was in Long Kesh Prison and he didn't know anyone who would help him dig up his vegetable patch so he could plant some potatoes.

So the old man wrote a letter to his son, who wrote back:

"Dad – whatever you do, don't dig in the garden! That's where I buried the guns."

The next day at 5 am, 20 British soldiers arrived and dug up all of the garden. They found no guns.

The old man was very confused about it all, and wrote to his son, asking him to explain what had happened and for advice on what to do next.

His son wrote back:

"Dear Dad,

Just plant your spuds."

What does a single yellow line in the road outside Stormont mean?
No parking at all.

What does a double yellow line outside Stormont mean?
No parking at all, at all.

Nuns and Priests

Two nuns are driving down a road late at night when a vampire jumps onto the bonnet of their car. The nun who is driving says to the other nun, "Quick! Show him your cross."

So the other nun leans out of the window and shouts, "Get off our feckin car."

127

What goes black and white, black and white, black and white?
A nun rolling downhill.

A priest and a nun are on their way back from the seminary when their car breaks down.

The garage doesn't open until the next morning so they have to spend the night in a B & B and it only has one room available.

The priest says, "Sister, I don't think the Lord would object if we spend the night sharing this one room. I'll sleep on the sofa and you have the bed."

"I think that would be fine," agrees the nun. They prepare for bed, say some prayers and settle down to sleep.

Ten minutes pass, and the nun says, "Father, I'm very cold."

"OK," says the priest, "I'll get a blanket from the cupboard."

Another ten minutes pass and the nun says again, "Father, I'm still terribly cold."

"Don't worry," says the priest, "I'll get up and fetch you another blanket."

Another ten minutes pass, then the nun murmurs softly: "Father I'm still very cold. I don't think the Lord would mind if we acted as man and wife just for a night."

"You're right," says the priest. "Get your own blankets."

A cop pulls over a car load of priests who are in America for an educational and instructional visit. The cop says "Father, this is a 70 mph highway. Why are you going so slow?"

The priest replies, "Sir, I saw a lot of signs that said 22, not 70."

The cop answers, "Oh, Father, that's not the speed limit, that's the name of the highway you are on! But, say, you sound

Irish, so if you're a visitor, I won't book you. My grandparents were Irish."

The priest says, "Oh! How silly of me! Thanks for letting me know. But surely there is no limit on driving slowly in the US?"

The cop shrugs, and says, "Well, you might get hit by some of these nuts, and it just ain't safe."

At this point, he looks in the backseat where the other priests are ashen-faced and clearly shaken. The cop asks, "Excuse me, Father, what's wrong with your friends back there? They're trembling!"

The priest answers, "Well, officer, we just got off Highway 101."

The chief priest of a seminary in America tells the two new priests that their first task is to paint their room without getting any paint on their clothes. So the one priest says to the other, "Hey, let's take all our clothes off, fold them up, and lock the door."

So they do this, and begin painting their room. Things are going well until they hear a knock at the door.

"Who is it?" one calls.

"Blind woman!"

The priests exchange glances, then one priest says, "She's blind, she can't see. What could it hurt?" They shrug and let her in.

The blind woman walks in and says, "Hey, Fathers! Nice pecs! Where do you want me to hang the blinds?"

One night a blonde Irish nun was praying in her room when she had a vision. God appeared before her.

"My daughter, you have pleased me greatly. Your heart is full of love for your fellow creatures and your actions and prayers are always for the benefit of others. I have come to you, not only to thank and commend you, but to grant you anything you wish," said God.

"Dear Heavenly Father, I am perfectly happy. I am a bride of Christ. I am doing what I love. I lack for nothing material since the Church supports me. I am content in all ways," said the nun.

"There must be something you would have of me," said God.

"Well, there is one thing," she said.

"Just name it," said God.

"It's those blonde jokes, and those Irish jokes. They are so demeaning to blondes and Irish people everywhere, not just to me. I would like for blonde and Irish jokes to stop."

"Consider it done," said God. "Blonde jokes and Irish jokes shall be stricken from the minds of humans everywhere. But surely there is something that I could do just for you."

"There is one thing. But it's really small, and not worth your time," said the nun.

"Name it, please," said God.

"It's the M & Ms," said the blonde Irish nun. "They're so hard to peel."

A rather grumpy priest was seated next to an Irishman on their flight home.

Soon after the plane was airborne, the stewardess came up the aisle to take drink orders. The Irishman asked for an Irish whiskey. The stewardess placed the drink on his tray and then asked the priest if he would like a drink. He replied loudly and indignantly, "I'd rather be savagely ravaged by brazen hussies than let alcohol touch my lips."

The Irishman then handed his drink back to the attendant and said "Me too. I didn't know we had a choice!"

The priests were chatting. "You know, since the warm weather started, I've been having terrible trouble with the mice in my church. I've tried everything – traps, bait, cats, spray, nothing seems to get rid of them."

Father O'Hara agreed, "My church, too. There are hundreds upon hundreds of them living in the crypt. I've set traps and even called in exterminators, but they're still there. Nothing has worked."

Father O'Leary joined in, "I had the same problem last year so I baptised the lot of them as members of my parish and haven't seen one of them since."

Father O'Malley's phone is ringing.

He answers it.

"Hello, is that Father O'Malley?" came the voice.

"It is."

"This is the Inland Revenue, tax department. Can you help us, perhaps?"

"I can."

"Do you know a Seamus T Murphy?"

"I do."

"Is he a member of your congregation Father?"

"He is."

"Can you recall, did he donate €20,000 to your church roof appeal?"

"He will."

Popes

Looking for a fresh marketing opportunity for his fried chicken company the owner calls the Pope and asks a favour:

"I want you to change the Lord's Prayer from 'Give us this day our daily bread' to 'Give us this day our daily chicken'. If you do it, I'll donate £10m to the Vatican."

"I'm sorry," the Pope replies, "it's the Lord's Prayer and I can't change it."

After another month of poor sales, the owner panics and calls again.

"Your Holiness, I really need your help. I'll donate £50m if you change the words to 'Give us this day our daily chicken'."

"Your offer is very tempting," the Pope says. "The church could do a lot of good with that much money. It would help us to support lots of charities. But again I must decline. It is the Lord's Prayer and I just can't change the words."

The owner hangs up again. After two

months of woeful sales, he is increasingly desperate.

"Your Holiness, here is my final offer. If you change the Lord's Prayer for me I will give £100m to the Vatican."

"Let me get back to you," the Pope replies. He calls together all his cardinals and says, "I have some good news and some bad news. The good news is that a fried chicken company is going to donate £100m to the Vatican. The bad news is that we've lost the bread account."

Jimmy from Glasgow is visiting Rome for a stag weekend and takes the bet, while under the influence, that he will blag his way into the Vatican and meet the Pope.

There is a huge uproar from the boys about this, but Jimmy, a determined young man, with the gift of the gab, takes the challenge.

By the following morning he has used

the contacts of his brother, a priest in Glasgow, to get into the Vatican.

By 10 am, he is negotiating for a new piping band to visit Rome in six months to play for Glasgow and show off their talent. The Pope's clerics are delighted, and invite him to meet the Pope.

Overwhelmed, Jimmy accepts and as the Pope appears on the balcony beside Jimmy who is waving to his mates below in St Peter's Square, one open-mouthed pal snaps a pic on his mobile and sends it to Jimmy's friends back in Glasgow.

Jimmy's pals gather around to admire the pic, dismayed only by Doris from London, who calls out, "That's a great shot of Jimmy, but who's the one in the white dress?"

 **Working Life**

Last year, Kevin, a young Irishman, got a job with a street-repair gang in London, in a central London borough which had just won "The Most Appalling, Deepest, This-Will-Kill-All-Cyclists, Pothole of the Year Award" for the two hundredth year in a row.

On his first day, Kevin turned up for work, and the repair gang, who all turned out to be Irish also, were singing "Happy Birthday" around the foreman.

"Is it the foreman's birthday?" asked Kevin.

"No, Kevin," came the reply. "It's the third anniversary of this pothole."

Seamus bumps into Patrick, after some months.

"Sure and you haven't been around for weeks now, Patrick. What is it you are up to?"

"Well, I've been keeping bees," replied Patrick.

"Well, then, me too," says Seamus. "I'll be keeping ten hives, each with 200 bees, and I get the great honey, you know!"

"Ach, that's nuttin'," boasts Patrick. "I'll be keeping five hives, each with 2,000 bees!'

"FIVE HIVES EACH WITH 2,000 BEES!" shouts Seamus. "Are you insane, man!

That's cruelty to animals! You'll get locked up, so you will!"

"Ach," replies Patrick. "Away! They're only feckin bees."

Michael O'Leary got a new car. It wasn't just a car – it was a super-fast, specially imported Lamborghini from Italy, and didn't he just think he was now a Formula One driver.

So he took the key excitedly, jumped in and roared off out of Dublin to see what his car was made of. He opened it up on the country roads and was soon heading down for Wexford at a roaring speed. He made it round really tricky, winding bends and was proud of both his skills and his car with its racing curves and the way it cornered.

Meanwhile, down the road, unknown to him, was an old farmer, Kevin O'Donoghue. Kevin and his farmhand, Patrick Fitzpatrick, were loading up the cart and the horse, Meg 2, to take them into market day in Wexford. This was a slow process, as Meg 2 had to be fed the farmer's sweetest hay before she would move. Finally, with the cart loaded up and the old farmer and his farmhand with their caps on, the reins were taken up and Meg 2 trotted calmly out of the large farmyard into the twisting road to Wexford.

As they turned out of the farmyard into the road, Michael O'Leary's car roared around the corner straight into the path of Meg 2, the cart and Kevin and Patrick. Always proud of his quick thinking, Michael handbraked left into the nearest entrance, narrowly avoiding hitting the farmers and Meg 2, the cart and its load.

The car came to a sudden stop in the old farmer's carefully stacked sweet hay, and then burst into flames. Michael O'Leary jumped out of the car to safety, and watched his car burn with the intensity of a Texan oilfield.

From the road, with the smell of burning hay and car in their nostrils, the farmers had a bird's-eye view of all that was happening.

They looked on in horror and in amazement as Michael O'Leary, shaken and in a state of disbelief, watched his car burning.

Then Kevin O'Donoghue and Patrick Fitzpatrick looked at each other, wide-eyed, and Kevin O'Donoghue said, "Well and sure, didn't we just get out of there in the nick of time!"

A doctor says to his patient, "I have bad news and worse news."

"Oh dear, what's the bad news?" asks the patient.

The doctor replies, "You only have 24 hours to live."

"That's terrible," says the patient. "How can the news possibly be worse?"

The doctor replies, "I've been trying to contact you since yesterday."

"It is impossible to enjoy idling thoroughly unless one has plenty of work to do."
(Jerome K Jerome)

Mick was being interviewed for the Golf Club's book-keeper's job by the Secretary.

Secretary: If I give you two rabbits and then I give you another two rabbits, how many rabbits do you have?

Mick: Five.

Secretary: No, listen carefully again. If I give you two rabbits and then I give you another two rabbits, how many rabbits have you got?

Mick: Five.

Secretary: Let's try this another way. If I give you two bottles of whisky and then I give you another two bottles of beer, how many bottles have you got?

Mick: Four.

Secretary: Good! Now, if I give you two rabbits and then I give you another two rabbits, how many rabbits have you got?

Mick: Five.

Secretary: How is it that two lots of two rabbits is five?

Mick: I've already got one rabbit at home!

Soon after O'Brien arrived at work, the Boss called him over and told him that he had a phone call in the front office. When he returned, he had a sad and tearful expression on his face and his head hung low. The Boss noticed and asked if it was bad news.

"To be shure it was, Boss," O'Brien replied. "I just found out that my mother died earlier this morning."

"Gosh, that's awful," replied the Boss, "Do you want the rest of the day off?"

"No," replied O'Brien wearily. "I'll finish the day."

About an hour later, the Boss called him over to tell him that there was another phone call for him in the office. This time when O'Brien returned he looked twice as glum, and the Boss asked if everything was all right.

"Boss, it's even worse news. That was my brother and he says his mother died today too!"

 **General**

What does an agnostic, dyslexic insomniac do?
Stays up all night and wonders if there is a dog.

What does an Irish, agnostic, dyslexic, insomniac do?
Stays up all night and worries if there was a dog, if he'd be Protestant or Catholic.

In the land of mists and rainbows, Ireland was the place for infamous wakes, many of which are now legend.

Those were the days when a wake would last days, or one at least, and when the body was placed in the middle of the room, and writers such as Synge and Shaw and Flann O'Brien wrote short stories and plays about them and retired on the untaxed profits …

So this joke is set in that time, when nostalgia was something to celebrate with rose-tinted glasses.

At the wake for Orla Phelan Juno Sheridan, who had died at the ripe old age of 104, the Sheridan family got the party started but at such a wake it was essential for everyone to do a turn as the day turned into evening, and the night began to go with a swing. Soon the entire room was jumping as Mary O'Brien danced an Irish jig – the 1950s equivalent of something from *Riverdance* – and many, including a wrestler, were brought to tears when wee Jimmy Brennan sang "Danny Boy". Mary Kenny told jokes, and Niamh Fitzgerald did some acrobatic manouevres that brought the wrestler sidling over to her side and asking her out.

Eventually only Bernard O' Connor, with his hands in his pockets, had not done a turn. The room turned to Bernard and called on him to perform.

"Away now," he cried, "I am not talented in any way, and can neither sing, nor dance, nor tell a joke. You carry on without me, please."

But this brought uproar in the room, and Bernard was not going to get away without a performance. After some thought, he said, "All right, then, I'll do a trick!" So everyone gathered round, and waited.

"What do I have in my pocket?" he called.

There was a long pause, and then a voice called out, "A packet of cigarettes!"

"No!" cried Bernard O'Connor. "The bulge in my pocket is not a cigarette packet."

He looked at the waiting, expectant, crowd and called out, "Well come on now! Have another guess."

"A deck of cards!" someone shouted.

"No, 'tis not a deck of cards," Bernard laughed. "Go on! Have another go!"

"Is it marbles?" called Mary Brennan with a giggle (for this was the 1950s when everyone was young and beautiful and innocent).

The room waited, with baited breath, listening for the answer.

"Another guess?" Bernard tempted them.

"Go on and tell us!" shouted the wrestler.

"'Tis me balls!" Bernard yelled.

The whole crowd roared, and the wrestler, who objected to foul language,

grabbed Bernard by the scruff of the neck, dragged him across the room and ejected him out of the door. He walked back in, brushing his hands and then saw Kevin's hat, which had fallen off in the scuffle. The wrestler grabbed the hat and strode across the room, throwing the hat out of the door after Bernard, who lay spread-eagled on the ground outside the house.

It was an hour later when the wrestler and some others, with several more drinks on board, realised Bernard was still outside.

Mary Brennan asked, "Can we not ask him back in, the poor soul? I'm sure the fella did not really mean it. Sure he's lying out there in the dust with his hat over him."

So the wrestler went back outside, helped Bernard to his feet and hauled him back in.

After an hour or so, when everyone in the room had done a turn, and everyone was too far gone to care, it came round to Bernard again.

"Which trick will you do?" said Natasha Roche.

The crowd roared, "Sing a song!"

"Tell a joke!"

"Do a jig!"

"No, no, no, I will do a trick!" Brendan cried.

So everyone at the wake paused, and waited. There was a buzz of drunken anticipation humming through the waiting crowd.

"Guess what's in me pocket?" cried Brendan.

"Is it a banana?" cried Barry Boyle.

"No, 'tis not a banana!" Brendan replied.

"Is it a large box for your fishing flies?" cried Ryan Roche.

"No! 'Tis not a large box for me fishing flies!" shouted Brendan.

"Is it a carriage clock nicked from the house of the dead?" shouted Paddy Power.

"No, most certainly it is not a carriage clock at all! Nor is it nicked from anyone! Oh, go on, I'll tell ya – 'tis me balls – again."

Brendan paused as the room hushed and groaned.

"I'll get me hat!" says he, running from the room and grabbing his hat from the hatstand on his way out.

Paul, an Irishman, was called from his hometown in Kerry for a key interview at a leading software company in California. His family had been amazed when he successfully completed all the online tests, and they couldn't believe he might soon be working in the Silicon Valley, making a fortune.

Once the main interview was over, he was told he had to complete one final test, which was in lateral thinking. Paul had always prized himself as a lateral thinker, so he felt the job was almost his.

He sat down with the interviewer in a different room with a view over a hot, sunny, landscape. Then he was given a piece of paper. On it were six horizontal lines printed in pairs. The interviewer asked if Paul could turn the six lines into nine.

Paul thought for a moment, turned the piece of paper round and, with a pencil, drew big bunches of leaves on the pairs of lines. Then he handed the paper back to the interviewer.

The interviewer looked at the paper and then at Paul.

"How do you get to nine here?" he asked.

"Well," said Paul, in his broad Irish accent, "tree plus tree plus tree adds up to nine."

"I see," said the interviewer. He pushed the piece of paper back to Paul across the desk and asked him to see if he could find a way to make ninety-nine.

Paul thought this over for a minute, then coloured in the lines, and handed it back to the interviewer.

"Yeah ... " said the interviewer. "You gonna explain to me please how you get to ninety-nine?"

"Well," said Paul. "Dirty tree plus dirty tree plus dirty tree makes ninety-nine."

The interviewer scratched his head and said, "Well, OK! So you gonna take the paper back and show me how to make one hundred?"

Paul thought this over and chewed the pencil for a while, and then finally drew a blob under each of the three pairs of lines and pushed the paper back to the bemused interviewer.

The interviewer, who had kept his Californian cool so far, looked exasperated. "How on earth do you make that one hundred?" he asked.

"Well, it's like this," said Paul, smiling. "Dirty tree and a turd, dirty tree and a turd, and dirty tree and a turd make one hundred."

The phone rang in Seamus's house.

"Hello?" says he.

"Oh, hello," said the voice on the other end of the line. "Is that Dublin two-two, two-two, two-two?"

"Oh, no, it is not!" replied Seamus. "I'm so sorry about that. This is Dublin double two, double two, double two."

"Ach, wrong number! Silly me! I am sorry to have troubled you," said the voice at the other end of the line.

"That's OK," answered Seamus. "The phone was ringing anyway."

Patrick bought his wellies on a terrible day of weather in September, but after wearing them for only one, wet morning, he reappeared, shuffling into the ironmonger's looking very frustrated.

The shop assistant looked at his beleaguered face, and asked what on earth was wrong.

"'Tis these wellies," Patrick wailed.

"What's wrong with the wellies?" said the shop assistant, looking down at Patrick's feet.

"I can't get going at all," moaned Patrick. "I need a bigger pair so the string is longer!"

"Ach, away," said the exasperated shopkeeper. "Away! The string is to keep them together when you are NOT wearing them!"

O'Donnell was far from handsome, and then he had bad luck in business and his wife and children left him. Very down on his luck, O'Donnell became depressed and decided there was no way out for him. So he drove to remote countryside, far from home, and stood by a train line, ready to jump and end it all.

Suddenly, he sensed that someone was standing behind him. Turning round, he jumped when he saw a wizened old leprechaun.

"Oh, you'll be having a bad day. Don't jump," the old leprechaun said. "Have three wishes instead!"

"Right," said O'Donnell. "I have nuttin' to lose. Can I have a million Euros please?"

"No trouble!" said the leprechaun. "You will have that money in your account tomorrow."

"Really!" said O'Donnell. "Well, for me second wish, I'd like my wife and kids to be at home when I get there please."

"No trouble," said the little leprechaun. "They'll be at home when you get back tonight!"

"Thank you," said O'Donnell.

"And for your third wish?" the old leprechaun said.

"Please can I be tall and handsome?" said O'Donnell.

The old leprechaun nodded and said, "When you get back to your car, and look in your mirror, you will find that your wish has been granted."

O'Donnell looked incredulous.

"But," said the leprechaun, "there is a little something I want you to do in return for me. I want you to kiss me."

O'Donnell shuddered, looked at the railway line, shrugged, and thought that under the circumstances, he might just as

well do as the old leprechaun asked. He leaned down to the puckered-up lips of the wizened little leprechaun, avoided his wizened old mouth, and pecked him on the cheek.

"What age are you?" the leprechaun said, clearly upset with the paucity of the kiss.

O'Donnell replied, "I'm forty."

"Well!" said the leprechaun. "Don't you think that you're a bit too old to be believing in leprechauns?"

Ryan was arrested for grievously assaulting a man. He was put into a line-up, in an identification parade with eight other men and the victim came into the room with police. Ryan started pointing and shouting, "That's him! That's him! Oi'd recognise him anywhere!"

Father Murphy walks into a pub in Donegal, and says to the first man he meets, "Tell me! Do you want to go to Heaven?"

The man says, "I do Father."

The priest says, "Then stand over there against the wall."

Then the priest asks the second man he meets, "Do you want to go to Heaven?"

"Certainly, Father," answers the man.

"Then stand over there against the wall," says the priest.

Then Father Murphy walks up to O'Donovan and says, "Do you want to go to Heaven?"

O'Donovan says, "No, Father, I don't."

The priest says, "What! I don't believe this. You mean to tell me that when you die you don't want to go to Heaven?"

O'Donovan says, "Oh, when I die – I thought you were getting a group together to go right now."

Ryan O'Healy opened the morning newspaper and was amazed to see in the obituary column that he had died.

He grabbed the phone and dialled his best friend, Barry Connolly.

"Barry, have you seen the paper today?" he demanded. "They say I died!"

"Yes, I saw it!" replied O'Healy. "Where are you callin' from?"

MacDermot was taking his first-ever ride in a plane, having crewed his way across the Atlantic on a boat. Flying over the Rocky Mountains, he couldn't stop staring at the scenery below. The flight attendant handed him a piece of chewing gum.

"It's to keep your ears from popping at high altitudes," the flight attendant explained.

"Thank you kindly, sir," said MacDermot and got busy with it.

When the plane landed, MacDermot rushed up to the flight attendant.

"Sir!" he said. "I'm meeting me cousins right away. How do I get the gum out of me ears?"

Dillon worked at the timber yard for twenty years and all that time he'd been nicking the wood and selling it on. One day he woke up, and his conscience, which had been nagging away at him for some time, was very bad and he went to confession to repent.

He sat in the confession box and spoke in a whisper:

"Father. Hello, 'tis Dillon here. 'Tis fifteen years since my last confession and I've been stealing wood from the timber yard all these years," he mumbled to the priest.

"I understand, my son," said the priest.

"Can you make a novena?"
    Dillon said, "Father, if you have the plans, I've got the timber."

Kevin Egan was standing in front of Ryan's Bar when he saw a driverless car rolling slowly down the road. He ran to the car, jumped in, and pulled on the emergency brake with a jerk.

Egan got out and proudly said to the man approaching him, "I stopped it!"

"I know, you eejit!" said the man. "I was the one pushing it!"

"Hello, Aer Lingus?" said Brian Ahearne. "Could ye be tellin' me how long it takes to fly from Boston to Dublin?"

The voice on the telephone said, "I'll see, sir. Just a minute."

"Aah, that's fast. Thank ye," said Ahearne as he hung up.

Joe Roche's wife had been killed in an accident and the police were questioning Roche.

"Did she say anything before she died?" asked the sergeant.

Joe Roche gave the sergeant a long, wise, considering look. "She spoke without interruption for about 40 years," said the Irishman.

An Englishman, a Frenchman and an Irishman were in a pub talking about their children.

"My son was born on St George's Day," said the Englishman, proudly, "so we decided to call him George."

"That's a real coincidence," observed the Frenchman. "My daughter was born on

Valentine's Day, so we decided to call her Valentine."

"That's really incredible," remarked the Irishman. "Exactly the same thing happened with my son, Pancake."

"Hey Patrick! Do I hear you spitting in the vase on the mantelpiece again!" cried Patrick's wife from the kitchen.

"No, me beauty," shouted Patrick back, "but I'm getting closer all the time!"

A police constable pulls up two Irish drunks and says to the first, "Now then! What's your name and address?"

"I'm Bernard Daly, of no fixed abode," the first one slurs.

The policeman then turns to the second

drunk, and asks him the same question.

"Well," he answers, "I'm Ronan O'Rorraty, and I live in the flat above Bernard."

Patrick Donnelly was driving along the road one beautiful summer's day when Kevin, the local policeman, a pal of his, pulled him over.

"What's wrong, Kevin?" Patrick asked.

"Ach, don't you know, Patrick, that I've been following you down the road for the past ten miles."

"And why would you do that?" Patrick asked, very confused.

"Your wife fell out of the car ten miles back!" retorted Kevin.

"Ah!" roared Patrick. "The Lord be praised," he said with relief. "I thought I'd lost me hearing and gone deaf!"

Two Irishmen were walking home after a night out on the beer when a severed head rolled along the ground past them.

Finn picked it up and stared into its face, and then he said to Fiach, "Jez, that looks like Joe!"

To which Fiach replied, "No, Joe was taller than that!"

A German, an Irishman and an Englishman were caught drinking in Saudi Arabia.

The prison guard said to the Englishman, before giving him his punishment, "Under Saudi law you have been sentenced to thirty lashes after which you will be deported. Before the punishment, you are entitled to have something put on your back. What will you have?"

The Englishman asked for linseed oil, as he was a cricket fan. Then he was given his thirty lashes and deported.

Next came the German.

"Under Saudi law," said the prison guard, "you have been sentenced to thirty lashes after which you will be deported. Before your punishment begins, you are entitled to something on your back. What do you want?" the prison guard asked.

"Nothing!" said the German.

And after receiving his lashes, the German spat on the ground, swore at the prison guard and at the Irishman before being led towards a car for the airport.

The prison guard then came up to the Irishman and repeated, "Under Saudi law you have been sentenced to thirty lashes after which you will be deported. Before your punishment begins, you are entitled to something on your back. What would you like?"

"Oh," replied the Irishman, 'I'll have the German."

Sean the Englishman, Sean the Scotsman and Sean the Irishman turned up for the opening ceremony of the Olympics, hoping to buy tickets at the gate.

When they saw how tight the security was, they wondered about blagging their way in, but that didn't seem likely either, so they regrouped and tried to come up with a new plan. They decided to go for a walk around the perimeter of the stadium and in their wander, Sean the Englishman came upon some left-behind scaffolding. Picking up a length of it, he went back to the gate and introduced himself as "Thomson, the pole vaulter" and he was admitted.

Sean the Scotsman saw this and going to where Sean the Englishman had found the scaffolding he found a discarded sledge hammer.

"Hello," he announced at the gate, "I am here to compete for the UK. I am McKay the hammer." And he was admitted.

Sean the Irishman searched the same

site for over an hour and was ready to quit when suddenly he saw his means of entry. He grabbed a roll of barbed wire and presented himself at the gate.

"O'Henry, fencing," he announced.

What's the quickest way to a man's heart? Through his chest with a sharp knife.

What's the difference between a boyfriend
and a husband?
About ten minutes.

Why is it so hard for a girl to find a
man who is caring, kind, sensitive and
handsome?
Because those fellas already have
boyfriends.

Why do men fancy nuns?
Because they're virgins and men hate
criticism.

Murphy was doing some tiling on the fireplace in Captain Sinclair's mansion. He was much impressed by the moosehead over the fireplace. "Indeed," he said, "it is a beautiful animal, Captain Sinclair, bigger even than the great Irish deer, to be sure."

"Indeed, yes," said Sinclair, "that moose was a fighter among moose. I tracked him for a week and when I finally shot him it took six men to load him onto the truck."

Murphy was impressed and said, "Truly, it is a great hunter that you are, Sir, and a great animal that was. Do you mind if I go into the next room and see the rest of him?"

Racehorse doping can be a problem in Ireland. One day, the Clerk of the Course spotted a trainer giving something to a horse just before the start of the first race. He went over and said, "Doping?"

The trainer said, "Indeed not, Sor. 'Tis just a lump o'sugar. Look, I'll taste a bit meself …see?"

The Clerk of the Course said, "Sorry, but we have to be careful. As a matter of fact, I like a bit of sugar meself." So the trainer gave him a lump.

When the Clerk of the Course disappeared, the trainer gave his jockey his last minute instructions.

"Don't forget the drill. Hold him in 'til the last two furlongs. Don't worry if anything passes ye, it'll be me or the Clerk of the Course!"

Mrs O'Toole was talking with her daughter about how she had changed as a mother from the first child to the last. She was explaining how she had mellowed a lot over the years.

"When your oldest sister coughed or sneezed, I called the ambulance. When your youngest brother swallowed a penny, I just told him it was coming out of his allowance."

Mick says to Seamus as they're walking home from the pub, "What a beautiful night, look at the moon."

Seamus stops and looks at Mick, "You are wrong, that's not the moon, that's the sun."

Both start arguing. Soon they come upon a real drunk walking the other way, so they stop him.

"Hello there, could you please help settle our argument?" says Mick. "Can you tell us what that thing is up in the sky that's shining. Is it the moon or the sun?"

The drunk looked at the sky and then looked back at them, and said, "Sorry lads, I don't live around here."

The Winter Olympics skater had just started his performance on the ice and slipped over on his backside. He recovered but then fell again, then again and again.

The judges gave their marks:

USA 0.0

UK 0.0

Switzerland 0.0

Ireland 4.4

"Why the score of 4.4?" the other officials asked the Irish judge.

"Well," he said, "you've got to make allowances. I mean it was terribly slippy out there!"

 **Wit and Wisdom**

Spanish singer Julio Iglesias was on television with British TV host Anne Diamond when he allegedly used the word "manyana". So Anne Diamond asked him to explain what "manyana" meant.

Julio Iglesias said that the term means "maybe the job will be done tomorrow, maybe the next day, maybe the day after that. Perhaps next week, next month, next year. Who cares?"

The host turned to Irishman Shay Brennan, the Manchester United and Ireland football star, who was also on the show, and asked him if there was an equivalent term in Irish.

"No," he replied. "In Ireland we don't have a word to describe that degree of urgency."

Overheard in a dining room, at breakfast, in a B & B in the Ring of Kerry, from the man cooking breakfast to a Liverpudlian visitor who was asking if the Peace Process was about land or religion:

"Jesus Mary Mother of God, why do ye have to bring religion into it?"

"It's not that the Irish are cynical. It's rather that they have a wonderful lack of respect for everything and everybody."
(Brendan Behan)

"I have a total irreverence for anything connected with society except that which makes the roads safer, the beer stronger, the food cheaper, and the old men and old women warmer in the winter and happier in the summer."

(Brendan Behan)

"New York is my Lourdes, where I go for spiritual refreshment ... a place where you're least likely to be bitten by a wild goat."

(Brendan Behan)

"A cigarette is the perfect type of pleasure. It is exquisite and leaves one quite unsatisfied. What more can one want?"

(Oscar Wilde)

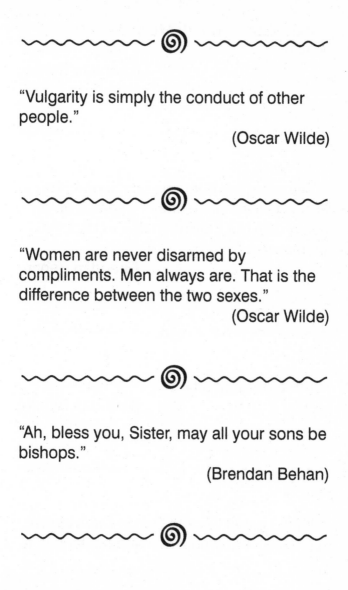

"Vulgarity is simply the conduct of other people."

(Oscar Wilde)

"Women are never disarmed by compliments. Men always are. That is the difference between the two sexes."

(Oscar Wilde)

"Ah, bless you, Sister, may all your sons be bishops."

(Brendan Behan)

"All publicity is good, except an obituary notice."

(Brendan Behan)

"Critics are like eunuchs in a harem; they know how it's done, they've seen it done every day, but they're unable to do it themselves."

(Brendan Behan)

"I am a daylight atheist."

(Brendan Behan)

"When I came back to Dublin I was court-martialled in my absence and sentenced to death in my absence, so I said they could shoot me in my absence."

(Brendan Behan)

"I am a drinker with writing problems."

(Brendan Behan)

"Ninety-seven saint days a year wouldn't affect the theatre, but two Yom Kippurs would ruin it."

(Brendan Behan)

"I wish I'd been a mixed infant."

(Brendan Behan)

"I have never seen a situation so dismal
that a policeman couldn't make it worse."
(Brendan Behan)

"If it was raining soup, the Irish would go
out with forks."
(Brendan Behan)

"I say myself no depressed words just
depressed minds."
(Brendan Behan)

Wit and Wisdom

"The most important things to do in
the world are to get something to eat,
something to drink and somebody to love
you."

(Brendan Behan)

~~~~~~~~~~ ◎ ~~~~~~~~~~

"It is a good deed to forget a poor joke."

(Brendan Behan)

~~~~~~~~~~ ◎ ~~~~~~~~~~

"One drink is too many for me and a
thousand not enough."

(Brendan Behan)

~~~~~~~~~~ ◎ ~~~~~~~~~~

"The Bible was a consolation to a fellow alone in the old cell. The lovely thin paper with a bit of matress stuffing in it, if you could get a match, was as good a smoke as I ever tasted."

(Brendan Behan)

"Other people have a nationality. The Irish and the Jews have a psychosis."

(Brendan Behan)

"Shakespeare said pretty well everything and what he left out, James Joyce, with a judge from meself, put in."

(Brendan Behan)

"The big difference between sex for money and sex for free is that sex for money usually costs a lot less."

(Brendan Behan)

"To get enough to eat was regarded as an achievement. To get drunk was a victory."

(Brendan Behan)

"We have always found the Irish a bit odd. They refuse to be English."

(Winston Churchill)

"The Irish gave the bagpipes to the Scots as a joke, but the Scots haven't seen the joke yet."

(Oliver Herford)

"When I get a very generous introduction like that I explain that I'm emotionally moved, but on the other hand I'm Irish and the Irish are very emotionally moved. My mother is Irish and she cries during beer commercials."

(Barry McCaffrey)

Praise the ripe field not the green corn.

(An Irish proverb)

"God invented whiskey to keep the Irish from ruling the world."

(Ed McMahon)

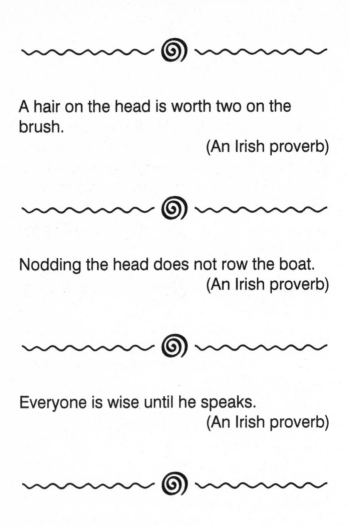

A hair on the head is worth two on the brush.

(An Irish proverb)

Nodding the head does not row the boat.

(An Irish proverb)

Everyone is wise until he speaks.

(An Irish proverb)

A son is a son till he takes him a wife, a daughter is a daughter all of her life.

(An Irish proverb)

Better be quarrelling than lonesome.

(An Irish proverb)

You never miss the water till the well has run dry.

(An Irish proverb)

I can resist everything except temptation.

(Oscar Wilde)

The Irish ignore anything they can't drink or punch.

(An Irish proverb)

"In Heaven there is no beer ...
That's why we drink ours here."

(A drinking song)

"Only Irish coffee provides in a single glass all four essential food groups: alcohol, caffeine, sugar, and fat."

(Alex Levine)